Two Winstons:

Conversations with My Grandchildren That Inspire
Questions That Lead to Independent Thinking

NANCY GRATTA

BALBOA.PRESS

A DIVISION OF HAY HOUSE

Balboa Press books may be ordered through booksellers or by contacting:

Balboa Press
A Division of Hay House
1663 Liberty Drive
Bloomington, IN 47403
www.balboapress.com
844-682-1282

Because of the dynamic nature of the Internet, any web addresses or links contained in this book may have changed since publication and may no longer be valid. The views expressed in this work are solely those of the author and do not necessarily reflect the views of the publisher, and the publisher hereby disclaims any responsibility for them.

The author of this book does not dispense medical advice or prescribe the use of any technique as a form of treatment for physical, emotional, or medical problems without the advice of a physician, either directly or indirectly. The intent of the author is only to offer information of a general nature to help you in your quest for emotional and spiritual well-being. In the event you use any of the information in this book for yourself, which is your constitutional right, the author and the publisher assume no responsibility for your actions.

Any people depicted in stock imagery provided by Getty Images are models,
and such images are being used for illustrative purposes only.
Certain stock imagery © Getty Images.

Print information available on the last page.

ISBN: 978-1-9822-5777-4 (sc)
ISBN: 978-1-9822-5778-1 (e)

Balboa Press rev. date: 11/12/2020

Contents

Dedication vii

Acknowledgement ix

Introduction xiii

Chapter 1 Two Winstons 1

Chapter 2 On Purple 7

Chapter 3 Fur Coat 13

Chapter 4 Fear of Fox 19

Chapter 5 The Rescue 25

Chapter 6 Horsey 31

In Conclusion 37

Dedication

To Virginia and Winston, the stars of the show

and to Ruthann, Peter, and Josh,

who made this book possible.

Thank you.

Acknowledgement

A special thank you to my friend and mentor, Diane Finn,

for your time, support and suggestions.

Questions unlock the answers that

are already within you.

"Gammy, do you know everything?" she asks.

"Yes," I reply honestly.

Introduction

What came first, the question or the answer?

I see it this way: There are traditional, long-standing questions, the who what where whys: Who am I? What is my purpose? Where did I come from? Why am I here? And there are questions that come from questions.

The more self-evolved, or self-aware, we become, the more questions we create to keep ourselves entertained as we weave through the educational process we call life. But where are the answers to those questions, you ask? Let's add children to the curriculum and find out!

When I first started writing the conversations with my grandchildren it was to remember the funny little moments we had together. I did not realize that these encounters would lead me to some very important questions and some very deep down discoveries about myself, about who I really am and why I think the way I do.

Meet Virginia. She is the most creative, original thinker I have ever met. In her mind every scrap of paper, every can, bottle, crayon or lump of clay is inspiration for an artistic masterpiece. And, unbeknownst to her and her family, she is a five year old Master Teacher.

Winston, her little brother by two years, is cut from a different cloth. His blue eyes always give hint to his on the fence kind of mischief or serious self. He's a focused architect when it comes to digging, hammering, taking apart, putting together, and inventing new lego contraptions. And he is a great defender for his work, his reasoning, and sometimes, even his sister.

So, welcome my friends, to the classroom we share together as we explore a journey to independent thinking.

I hope you will be inspired to honor the children in your life for the teachers that they are and the wisdom they posses. May your observations and your interaction lead to questions that bring excitement to your life and answers that bring peace to your heart.

Many blessings,
Nancy

Chapter One

Two Winstons

"Winston, want to see the video I took of you outside?" I ask.

"Come sit next to Gammy."

I don't know why I sometimes talk about myself in the third person, but Winston understood and came to sit beside me on the step.

We had been outside a few minutes earlier. Winston ran around collecting things from the yard to fill up the bucket of his electric ride-on dump truck. Rocks, tree branches, sand toys, one item at a time, into the bucket. Anything and everything a treasure. He was adorable in his little boy bliss. Definitely worthy of a recording by his Grandmother.

Now inside, I want him to see the video.

"Look, Winston. That's you."

Winston looks at the image on my phone, at me, then again at the phone.

"There's two Winstons Gammy? There's a Winston outside?"

"No honey, that's you."

"He has a shirt just like me, Gammy?"

"No Winston, that's you. Gammy took a picture of you when we were outside. That's you, wearing your shirt."

"Can I go outside and say hi to him, Gammy?"

I have to admit I got a chuckle the first time I put this conversation on paper. I imagined Winston reading this in the years to come and thinking, as I did on that day, that he did not see the real picture. He was not seeing from my perspective. But, no worries, I rationalized, someday he will.

As I reflected on my first take on this conversation I began to question. Did I really want three year old Winston to adopt my thinking? After all, how many people think they are less open to their intuitive gifts as adults because they were shut off from them in their childhood? And why didn't I give room to Winston's perspective instead of trying to win him over to mine? Is this a critical moment in the development of Winston's independent thinking or am I just confusing the little boy?

Hmmm... Let me think. Is it really possible to see from someone else's perspective, or, to borrow a phrase "see through someone else's eyes"? As individuals we vary in physical brain function, life experience, environment, influences, and style of communication. We may have the same material make-up but we are each arranged in a very unique and personal way. Okay, so now I'm thinking it's impossible to see from someone else's perspective. You may be thinking something else entirely.

Deciding to move on from the literal question at hand I leave it like this: I see a snapshot in the life of Winston. Winston sees a little boy outside.

If we recognize the unique blend of characteristics that comprise individual perspective we might gain an understanding of our differences and let go judgment of ourselves and others. We could see from a new, collective viewpoint with love and compassion. Then we are no longer what we imagine ourselves or others to be. We simply BE.

Another line of thought generated from the exchange with Winston, my sweet little muse, has to do with timing in the development of perspective. Summed up and often repeated as, "All things happen in Divine Timing". Well, what exactly is Divine Timing?

Winston expressed his belief of the boy outside at the time of his three year old uniquely compiled and functioning self. At any moment his belief could change, because Winston himself changes, moment to moment, experience to experience.

We see things differently from a three year old perspective, or a twelve year old perspective, or that of a thirty year old. I am finding that the same story I've told to myself as a young person, or a middle aged adult, now appears very different to my sixty three year old self.

Now let's think about timing in regard to change and how that factors into perspective.

Perhaps you have a reoccurring thought, remembrance or synchronistic experience: something or someone that pops up at various times in your life. You may think, "I thought I was done with this long ago" or "I haven't thought about that person since high school, why am I thinking of him or her now?"

Here's why. The ability to utilize your brain function changes over time. Your varied life experience gives you a wealth of potential choices, and your perceived support or lack of support creates an influencing factor. Therefore, any healing or growth that occurs is connected to the ongoing writing and re-writing of the evolving script.

Simply put, you give to yourself what you can process at the time and in the way that makes sense to you. Each increment of time gives you new input and new perspective. And… a new opportunity to decide, to make a conscious choice, about your new perspective.

Because of our unique arrangement of self, everyone's Divine Clock is different. That is why the grieving process, the birthing process, the aging process, or any other process you work on or walk through, is accomplished on your own time card. You punch in and punch out at the time perfect for you. Yes, you're the worker, but the really good news is… you're the boss, too.

I hope Winston will hold on to his own perspective and continue to develop independent thinking. And, I hope that I will become even more aware of my interference, and instead, inquire about his thoughts, encourage his curiosity, and leave open the door of discovery.

So you see, Winston, my cute little box of questions, bucket filling, boy of pure genius, you are an inspiration. No kidding.

Chapter Two

On Purple

"How was your day?" I ask Ginny.

"Purple!" she exclaims, jumping from ottoman to couch to chair, and back again, like a little jumping bean. "Purple, purple, purple!"

"Ok. That's great," I say, my head moving back and forth to keep pace with each jump. "What does that mean?"

"If you're really, really good you get on purple," she explains, still in motion.

"If you're only sort of good you get green."

"Ok." I say again, "So you were really, really good today. What did you do that was so really, really good?"

"I helped another kid clean up the toys."

"Well, you are a really, really good helper, at school and at home" I say, hoping that purple feeling will spill over into a help- Gammy- pick- up-the- house- before- Mom- and- Dad- get- home kind of activity. It doesn't, but then all that being good at school combined with all that jumping at home make a girl pretty tired. I get it.

The next day Ginny comes home "on green". "But it's bright green," she explains. "That's the best kind of green you can get."

"What did you do to get bright green?" I ask.

"Well…" she begins, giving me the 'you should know this' head tilt, "I didn't get in any mistakes."

"Oh, that's good," I say.

"Did you ever have any mistakes when you were a kid, Gammy?"

"Oh, yeah," I reply, "lots and lots of mistakes. Kids make lots of mistakes and then they learn how to do things, or they learn more about things. I made lots of mistakes when I was a kid."

I wasn't worried about saying this to her because, first of all it was true, and secondly I knew that Ginny would not try to follow in my footsteps but continue to try her five year old best. I hoped it would give her a little balance.

Ginny comes home each day with a report of purple or green. She informs me that on purple days she may color one of the shapes in her kindness bucket. When all the shapes are colored she walks, by herself, to the school's treasure chest and exchanges her bucket for a toy. Obviously, to her, this is a very big deal.

One day Ginny arrives home with a little plastic horse in the palm of her hand, the kind you might get in a five-cent gumball machine if they were still around. She loves horses, not to ride I am told, but to train. Someday she will be a famous horse trainer.

"So I guess you're on purple," I say to her as I admire the horse.

"Yeah," she replies, "Some kids ended up on yellow. One kid is on red."

From Ginny's description it seems that the teacher wipes the slate clean each afternoon and the next day every child begins on the same color, sometimes bright green or just green, and sometimes purple. The children can stay on the appointed color or go up or down accordingly, depending on their behavior.

Ginny tells me one little boy usually ends each day on red.

"What does he do to get red?" I ask.

"Well," she sighs, "he talks or he doesn't sit in the circle. Sometimes he distracts other kids. Then he gets on yellow. If he keeps it up he goes to red."

"What's his name?" I ask and she tells me.

"That's a nice name," I say.

"What are some of the other kids' names in your class?" I ask and Ginny replies, as she gallops the little horse across the kitchen table,

"I don't know yet, Gammy. I'm still just learning them."

If questions are a path to knowledge, then discussion and action generated from the questions lead to wisdom. What do you think?

Will Ginny's constant strive to be "on purple" turn her into a perfectionist? Was that a trait already there? Are we encouraging her in this direction, affecting her self-esteem, or in some way adding stress to her already learning to adjust-and- conform kindergarten journey?

And what about the little boy "on red"? Is his reputation and his self expectation being solidified? If so, will this be impeding or motivating? Will he embrace this role? If so, in what way, and for how long?

How does participation in this system influence a child's thoughts of him/herself in regards to their sense of belonging or isolation? Their sense of achievement or pride? What about the fact that each child's development is played out in front of the other children? Does this encourage comparison? Competition?

It might seem that, in asking these questions, I am passing judgment. I am trying not to. I am trying to observe, not judge. There is a difference. I recognize that it must be challenging, indeed, for a teacher with twenty-four five year olds in a classroom, to impart information to the precious little ones, organize, keep safe, evaluate, AND assign each child a color throughout the day. Teachers are super human super heroes. Truly.

Could this color system be a microcosm of the macrocosm? It helps me wonder how much of who we are is determined by the expectations of our family, teachers, culture and customs. What about birth order, DNA and physical attributes? Or our experiences in life and love, circumstance and maybe even… luck? Is there a personal evolution in this lifetime or a composite of many lifetimes?

Who am I and how did I get here?

Perhaps these questions were once pondered on the steps of Socrates' classroom or under a tree with Buddha. Or maybe Popeye had the big answer after all when he said, "I yam what I yam, and dats all what I yam."

Well, anyway, Ginny may be "on purple" at school but she might be nearing yellow jumping on furniture at home. And, maybe, the little boy in her class has his own color schedule. I hope so. All I know, so far, is that Ginny knows his name.

Chapter Three

Fur Coat

It's October and the mornings are sometimes pretty chilly. It warms as the day goes on and the sun shines and it ends up feeling like early fall or late summer. So layers are the way to go.

Virginia, she likes to be called Ginny, has four weeks of kindergarten under her belt and is pretty up to speed on the morning drill. Breakfast, teeth, get dressed, brush hair while watching a show on her computer, and a final craft project if she can squeeze it in before the bus comes.

Ginny is allowed to choose her outfit of the day and usually, except for gym day when sneakers are a must or you're sidelined, there are no adult revisions.

For days on my watch, Ginny asks to wear her white fur coat. It is a beautiful coat, the kind perfectly suited for the velvet Thanksgiving dress with matching bow. "No," is my answer. "It's not cold enough for that coat yet," is my reasoning.

On Friday morning it is especially cold as we head out the door for the bus. I mean really cold, like actual winter cold. Ginny steps one foot out the door, realizes her opportunity, and back in again.

"Gammy. It's freezing! I'm freezing! Please, please, please can I wear my white coat?"

Well… it is freezing.

"Ok," I say, finally giving in.

Ginny opens, then disappears behind, the double doors of the mudroom closet. A few too many seconds pass and I know something's up.

She emerges in full outfit, beautiful white fur coat and beige knitted hat with huge pom-pom on top. She raises her hands in the air, palms toward me, to show off an oversized pair of driving gloves with no-slip grips. Where did these come from I wonder? I am about to say she looks like a roly-poly little snowman and renege on my coat decision but I see her happy, "what do you think of this great find" expression and I hesitate for just a moment.

Ought oh, too late. The bus is coming. No time for discussion. At least she's warm, I think to myself. After all, it is freezing out here.

The bus stops, the door slides open, and Karen, the driver, greets us with her "morning is great" smile. I love Karen and I enjoy and appreciate her approach to each new day. Kindergarten, bus ride, Ginny blowing me kisses…it really is true. Morning is great.

Karen has not seen enough at first glance to get a good impact. Ginny reaches up with her little hands inside the big gloves and grabs the safety railings on each side of the doorway. She hoists herself gallantly onto the first step. Good so far. Looking good, Gin. Good and warm.

As she makes her move for the second step something goes wrong. The glove on her right hand sticks to the safety railing. Like Velcro tearing apart, she rips it away and is free. She tries to advance and now the left glove sticks. Slowly she progresses… stick… rip… step up. Stick… rip… step up. All the way, adorably determined, she makes it to the top and slides into her seat in the first row.

All this time, which seems like minutes to me, and probably hours to Ginny, I am doubled over, laughing. Karen is laughing, too. The more Karen and I look at each other laughing, the more we laugh. Ginny is not laughing. She is looking at me from her little bus window. No smiles, no blowing kisses, her eyes locked on mine, glaring, as the bus pulls away.

All day long I think of that little girl and how much I adore her. I feel so guilty. I am a bad, bad Gammy. And all day long I laugh every time I replay the morning scene in my mind.

In the afternoon I am super early at the bus stop, thinking that, in my mind at least, I can repair my status to Good Gammy. I am hoping that the rest of Ginny's day was spectacular, making up for the morning challenge and the part I played in my granddaughter's suffering.

The bus stops. The doors open. Karen and I try not to look at each other.

"I smiled the whole day," I say to her.

"Me, too," Karen says, both of us trying hard to put on our adult faces.

Ginny jumps her way down each step. It's now about 75 degrees and she is wearing her tee-shirt and jeans. I'm hoping that her fur coat and the pom- pom hat are scrunched up in her little backpack. I don't even want to think about the gloves. It doesn't matter. I don't ask.

As means to redeem myself and also get a read on how the day went I say,

"You were so cute this morning. You made Karen and Gammy smile the whole day. How was school?"

"It was awesome, Gammy. It was flashlight Friday!"

"Thank God, thank God for flashlight Friday," I say in my head, not knowing what flashlight Friday is but silently thanking Mrs. O'Halloran for her end of the week special project.

My heart bursting with joy and my conscience somewhat clear, I think how easily, and sometimes unknowingly, we touch each other's lives and how precious this connection.

I know that what I say and do has an impact in some way on my granddaughter. It might be a little impact, like changing the mood when singing in the car. Or a medium impact, when turning a perfectly wonderful day into Ginny's "worst day ever in my whole life I'm never coming out of my room …and I am not changing my attitude" kind of day, when told she cannot play with the umbrella inside the house.

And, I know that I can also impact in a very big way. It doesn't have to be with words. Thank goodness, as I'm hoping that at least fifty percent of the overly protective grandmother things I say might be forgotten. My greatest impact on Ginny comes from who I am, from just being me… from just being.

An example of impact comes to mind as I think of Vovo.

I went to her funeral last week. Vovo was a cute little, eighty eight year old Portuguese woman. In her life she was a girl, a wife, a mother, a grandmother, a great-grandmother, a worker in a cafeteria, a friend, a neighbor, and more. From the stories that were told she was not a perfect person, but perfectly her. She didn't always say the nicest things. She liked to do things her own way, in her own time and could be a bit frustrating to others. She cuddled children, read books, cooked meals, told stories, yelled, cried, and laughed lots. And, she had a great big heart. At the wake people stood in line for more than an hour to pay their respects. The funeral procession was at least a mile long. Family, friends, co-workers, neighbors and others came to say good-bye, and most of all, thank you, to a little woman that made a great big impact in their lives.

As human beings we are continuously influenced and influencing, yet we may never know the extent to which we affect others. I am sure Vovo was surprised, as she peeked in on us that day, to see the people and hear the stories they told about her. Just as Ginny will someday be surprised at the influence her five- year- old self made on her sixty- three- year- old grandmother.

Chapter Four

Fear of Fox

Small tufts of brown hair spike out in all directions, like a crown on the top of his head. He is wearing his favorite cozy outfit, red dinosaur shirt with grey sweatpants, and it sticks to his body in tiny wet patches. Little footprints trail behind him.

"Hi, Winston," I say, as we meet in the hallway.

Man on a mission, he looks up, surprised to see me.

"Gammy," he announces, a bit of mischief in his voice, "I'm afraid of two things."

"Two things?" I question, waiting for more.

"Yep," he replies with conviction, "tigers and vaginas."

Now, let me explain before we go further. As babies, Winston and his sister, Virginia, enjoyed a free-spirit kind of existence, romping in the ocean and changing on the beach. They asked appropriate childlike questions about anatomy and sexuality and their parents answered honestly, openly, and respectfully. I am not surprised that the words tiger and vagina are in Winston's vocabulary, I am simply confused to hear them paired together.

"Hmmm…," I say, trying to buy a bit of time. Teachable moment, teachable moment… I know you're in here somewhere.

"Ok," I begin, seeing him angle slightly away from me and sensing flight. "I can understand, if a tiger is coming down the road, you would be afraid and run away as fast as you could. But a vagina, that's just a girl part."

He stood still for a moment. "What are you talking about, Gammy?" Now we are both confused.

"You know, a girl has a vagina and girl parts, and a boy has a penis and boy parts," I continue.

A little pause, that's good. The wheels are turning now.

"Do all girls have vaginas?" he asks.

"Yes," I reply.

"Then, I'm afraid of all girls."

Oh, no. This conversation has taken a turn. Before I can change gears Winston asks, "Do you have a vagina, Gammy?"

"Yes, Winston." Then, trying to keep it simple, I add, "I'm a girl."

"No you're not."

"Yes I am."

"No you're not."

"Yes I am."

"No, … you're not." He says, now on the move.

"Yes, … I am." This is fun. I might actually win this round.

"Humph!," Winston sounds off, triumphant as he marches round the corner and into the toy room, "Then I'm afraid of you!"

Overhearing the conversation, Winston's mother enters the hallway and explains that I am not the first person he had shared these fears with. Apparently, he received a variety of responses. And, judging from his response to my response, I might not be the last.

Even if Winston was playing me, it did get me thinking.

Real or imaginary, fear is fear. Winston might really be afraid of tigers. But, what are the chances of one running down the street? And could he really outrun it? (As Winston's CNN source I may have added to his fear with that one.)

Fear can mobilize us or stop us in our tracks. It can help us soar to amazing heights when we overcome it, or crash us to the ground when it overcomes us.

And, if it's true that our thoughts create our reality, then fear might be the limiting factor in the manifesting equation. It can distort the process, put up a barrier, or sabotage the outcome.

Most people are afraid of something. Things, like spiders, or elevators. Or situations, like fear of failure, or of success, fear of commitment in a relationship, or of being alone. They might have a fear of lack- not having enough money, beauty, intelligence, or opportunity. Or the opposite, having too much.

Oh, come on, you might say. Who has a fear of having too much money? Think of the lottery. If you won a million dollars would you share it? Would everyone be happy for you? What if you won a hundred million dollars? How would you manage it, who would you trust? Could it put you or your family in danger? Perhaps fears around money affect income and establish a comfort zone. If we conquer our financial fears, do our chances of winning the lottery change?

We can work with fear and, this is the most important part, we have a choice with it. We can face it, identify it, ignore it, or get help for it. We can voice it, bury it, or use it to keep us safe. And, we can harbor it or send it packing.

Fear is an emotion with a purpose, a tool we can use to determine the direction we want to travel and the life picture we want to paint. It contributes to a multitude of miracles. You may have heard a story where a mother, fearing her child in danger, overcame what seemed the impossible and rescued the child. Most likely you have experience, where the result of fear, partnered with love, altered your life in some way. Fear, partnered with love. Amazing.

When dealing with fear, our thoughts and actions are as unique and individual as we are. We may be counseled, but there's no one-size-fits-all plan of mastery.

Winston's father, Josh, told him a story one night.

"I stepped outside," he began with a spooky voice. "It was very, very, dark. All of a sudden I saw a pair of bright red eyes, staring out from the woods. Then, another pair, and another, until there were six pairs of eyes. They were fox, a whole family of them, and they were looking right at me!"

"What happened?" Winston half-whispered, his full attention on his father's face.

"I stared them down." answered his father valiantly, then advised, "Never let them see your fear."

Well, I don't know much about facing fear and fox. Maybe Josh knows what he's talking about. After all, he is from Maine. And even if it is true, does it apply to tigers? What about vaginas?

Chapter Five

The Rescue

I walk in the door and Ginny grabs my hand to pull me into her bedroom. She wants to show me the collection of art projects made from her current bin of recyclables. Her inventive and imaginative pieces often remind me of pop sculptures, wind chimes, whirly gigs, and rusty iron monuments made from old car parts. Reminiscent of art you might see on a yard of tall grass in Vermont. This girl has artistic potential and I am excited to be invited into her studio to view her creations.

Today's menagerie includes paper towel tubes covered in glue with smiling faces, a family of little creatures made of stone, tissue paper, and googly eyes, and at the center of all this brilliance, the main attraction, an apple completely covered in clear push pins, reflecting the light and seeming like an amazing, blazing Christmas ornament. Ginny cannot contain her pride!

"Do you like it, Gammy?" she asks. "I worked on it all last night!"

"She did," her father confirms as he enters the room, Winston tagging behind him, blankie in tow, thumb in mouth. "I told Ginny about cloves and oranges thinking we could give that a try this weekend."

"But I like it this way," Ginny pipes in.

"It really is beautiful," I say. "Where did you get the pins?"

I gently pick up the object of admiration and turn it reverently around in the palm of my hand. The bottom of the apple is slightly brown and squishy but, not wanting to ruin the mood, I say nothing about this.

"You have to be careful of the pointy ends," I tell her as if she didn't discover this on her own last night.

"And, Winston," I say, eyeing the little guy eyeing the glittering ornament, "this is Ginny's art work. This is not a toy."

"Oookaaay," he says, not quite convincingly.

Later that day I busy myself with a load of laundry while the children busy themselves in play. Ginny runs into the laundry room, "Gammy, Gammy, come quick! There's a huge bug in my room and it's the stinging, biting kind."

"Ok." I say calmly. "Stay away from it and I'll be there in a minute."

"Ok." She says running back towards her room, "I'll keep my eye on it!"

Seconds later Ginny runs to me again. "Never mind, Gammy," She says puffing, out of breath, more from excitement than exertion, "Winston's taking care of it!"

Now I am paying attention. Ginny runs back to her room, this time with me at her heels.

Brave little Winston, brandishing a push pin and mustering all his energy into air chops and karate kicks hovers over a lethargic, or maybe dazzled into dazed, stink bug.

"Great rescue, Winston," I say. "Now I need two helpers to get this guy outside."

Gently, trying not to alarm the harmless but sleepy insect, we work together to guide the tiny body onto a Kleenex, parade it through the house and, with a little flourish, out the back door.

"Wow, Octonaughts, that was close." I say.

"Yeah," Winston sighs, and Ginny agrees, "That was close."

At some point or another everybody needs a hero. When Ginny asked me to don the cape for the bug rescue I wasn't available. Luckily, Winston stepped up to the plate.

Let's think about this. What is a hero? Do you have one? If not, how do you get one? And, is it possible that you just might be one?

I think a hero could be a person who has your back, so to speak. Maybe a parent, a best friend, or someone who is just in the right place at the right time for the right action… or, the right words.

When your hero is nearby you don't have to be the strong one. You can show your fear and not be judged for it. You might think your hero is stronger than you, a protector of sorts, but maybe your hero is someone who helps you recognize just how strong you are.

If you don't have a hero you can invent one or borrow one from a television show or a children's book. Like Superwoman or The Man with the Yellow Hat. Perhaps it is someone that will save you, or at least point you in a good direction, so that you can save yourself.

A hero can show you, through example, the kind of person you would like to be. They reflect back to you the values you admire. Your hero might be patient, kind, understanding and forgiving. Those seem like pretty good traits for a hero.

There may be different ingredients for different heroes and maybe the situation provides a clue as to who takes on that role and when. Ginny and Winston may fight as siblings, but look who showed up when needed.

It might feel good to have a hero or be one, especially when this having or being creates a balance of giving and receiving and a feeling of purpose and unity... when one heart connects in service to another. Is a hero one who steps in to remind us of the things we are most grateful for?

In my lifetime I've collected lots of names for my hero list, but clearly my everyday hero is my daughter, Ruthann. She is my best friend and my confident. I can tell her or ask her anything and she'll tell me truthfully what she thinks in the kindest way possible. She makes sure I have what I need, even though she has others who depend on her. I admire how she makes easy conversation with everyone and helps them feel welcome because she is genuine and truly interested in their story. Ruthann is brave, adventurous, loving and wise. And every single day, no matter what else is going on in her life, she has my back.

Chapter Six

Horsey

A warm glow streams through the window to wake me and I listen as little slipperd footsteps approach, and then stop, at the guestroom door.

"Good morning, Gin. You're up early."

She walks slowly into my bedroom, head down, pajamas rumpled. Usually a cheery late riser, it is easy to see that something is seriously amiss.

"What's wrong, baby girl?" I ask.

"I miss Horsey," she moans.

"I know," I reply sympathetically. I lift the blanket and pat the bed, a signal for her to snuggle in beside me.

Horsey was a pink square of soft fabric with satin ribbon edging, a little horse head on one side and a fluffy white tail on the other. She was a baby shower gift and, for Ginny, it was love at first sight. Horsey went everywhere with Ginny.

She was often In the carriage, in the car, at the mall doing errands or wrapped in a blanket by the pool for swimming lessons. To ensure a happy trip of any kind, her wise mother always checked Horsey aboard. And for five wonderful years Horsey was dragged, embraced, dressed, fed, repaired, and often, as Ginny slept, washed thoroughly.

"Do you think I will always miss her?" Ginny asks.

"Maybe, a little," I reply.

Horsey disappeared four months ago. Ginny had come from a visit with her dad, arriving home in tears and without her companion. A great search for a replacement Horsey began, but try as we might, there was none, and Ginny's grief continued.

"It's all my fault," she says now, pulling the blanket up to her chin, "I should have listened."

"What do you mean?" I ask.

"Daddy told me to leave Horsey in the car when we went to Uncle Jeremy's cabin. He said I might forget her," she begins, her eyes wet now. "But I took her out of the car anyway, and I let baby Maggie hold her. I only turned around for a minute but then she was gone. Everybody looked, but we couldn't find her."

Oh… For the first time I hear this part of the story and suddenly realize why the loss of this toy is so difficult for Ginny to bear. She feels sad and… she feels guilty.

I make an attempt to ease her burden and say:

"Well, when we love someone who's gone, we can make a special place for them in our heart. We can keep all our happy memories there. It's like having a little piece of them with you always."

Ginny sits up suddenly.

"But, I do have a piece of her, Gammy. Don't you remember? When you sewed her tail back on you cut off the tag. I kept it. It's in my jewelry box."

"You kept the tag?" I ask, astonished, forgetting for a moment that this little girl keeps just about everything. "Go get it."

Ginny jumps out of bed, runs up the stairs, and within minutes returns, label in hand, a tiny little piece of fabric…with the company name.

And, immediately, the journey of Horsey's reincarnation begins.

Later that day, for the third time, Ginny asks, "Do you think Horsey will come in the mail tomorrow?"

"No, Gin" I reply patiently, "Remember what the lady said."

"Ok, ok, ok," Ginny says, jumping up and down, "Don't you think it's a miracle, Gammy!"

I do think finding the new Horsey is a kind of miracle, or at least a very synchronistic chain of events. As a family we searched the internet and although we found dogs and cats, giraffes, elephants, bears, and even mice, there were no horses to be found. Ginny's remembrance of Horsey's tag led us to the company name, which led us to a phone number, which led us to a kind person who listened to our story and put the missing puzzle piece in place: The Horsey model was discontinued five years ago.

Then, patiently looking through past inventory while we hold the line, the young woman discovers there should be one.. yes, one... remaining Horsey in a bin at the back of the warehouse.

"When I find it I will send it to you," she says excitedly, endearingly becoming part of the story.

Over the next few days, Ginny asks lots of questions.

"Do you really think it will be Horsey, but just in a new body? Do you think she'll recognize me? Will she be mad at me for losing her first body?"

"Can the same thing happen to people, Gammy?" Ginny asks, taking my hand. "like when you die, can you get a new body?"

"Some people think it's possible." I say. "What do you think?"

"I think you can." Ginny says softly.

This is a story of a five year olds' grief for a toy. But, it's much more than that. It's about process.

When Ginny lost her beloved Horsey we tried to ease her sadness with a quick replacement. But Ginny didn't need a replacement just then, she needed time.

This was Ginny's first big encounter with loss. She needed to experience and process grief before she could share the deeper pain, the thought that she might be responsible for Horseys' disappearance.

When we lose a loved one grief and guilt may walk hand in hand. What if we had done something or said something differently? Would the outcome be different, our hurt less intense? Did we miss an opportunity to express love or gratitude or find closure?

Perhaps guilt helps us to explore our role in the story. Maybe once we process the what ifs and come to terms with them we can begin to heal.

So, healing, just like everything else, involves process.

Process is a step by step plan, written after the fact, and in disappearing ink, so that a person can re-write it with new specifications. It's personal and unique to the circumstance or individual. And, it involves time. And it evolves change.

Have patience with the process, trust the process. This is a hard thing to do when we are in the middle of the process, much easier in hindsight when we begin to feel a sense of peace, a flow, a new kind of existence.

Have faith in the process or just have faith. Faith is the key to existing when we don't have the answers to our questions. It's the remembrance of the potential to find what we need as time does its' job.

Ginny's story with Horsey has a happy ending. Together they traveled a road of loss and grief, questions and answers that led to more questions and answers, and letting go, at least a little. New Horsey has earned a place high on the favored list, perched on bed pillows and kissed each night. But now there's room for Perry and Winkle and a host of others who have found a perfect place in Ginny's heart, and, if I'm honest, in mine too.

In Conclusion

I remember a discussion I had with my college advisor, many decades ago, when I was preparing for my Master thesis.

"Choose another topic" she said sternly, "We've been over this."

"Why?" I asked, observing her frustration come to surface.

"Education doesn't work that way. Teachers do not have time to address every question from every student. It's not good to encourage that idea, especially at the elementary level. There just isn't time."

But, I didn't give up. I have always been aware that I learn best through question and answer, even if I hold the question to myself. And I witness others learning from this system as well. Learning through questions and answers is not a new idea. The Ancients used it. Historians, philosophers, and scientists- there isn't a person or a profession that hasn't learned in some way, from questions and answers. And, let's be sure about this, kids use it all the time. Always have and always will.

So, yes, I did write my thesis on learning through questions and answers. You knew that, right?

As a mother I encouraged my daughter to question, as well, and found very early on that as she questioned, I learned.

When Ruthann was in first grade I received a note from her teacher requesting a meeting. "Ruthann, why does your teacher want to talk to me?" I asked.

"I don't know, Mommy. Maybe I'm not coloring fast enough" she replied.

At the meeting Mrs. Hillary explained that Ruthann was taking too much time doing her work. She was overly concerned with doing it neatly. And, she was asking too many questions.

The teacher was not opposed to the questions, noting that some of them were quite good, it was just that it took up too much class time.

"Well, what shall we do about this?" I asked, the apple not falling far from the tree.

We agreed that Ruthann could ask one question on the topic at hand and if she had others she could write them in a special question notebook. The teacher or I would address them at the end of the day.

It turned out that some pretty brilliant questions missed the comprehension mark when communicated through a first graders writing and spelling ability. At the end of the day we couldn't decipher the original question.

But, Ruthann was happy, after awhile, just drawing in her special notebook. She discovered she could figure out some of the answers for herself and if she still had questions, she could ask. A win-win for the time being.

It is important to find someone to listen to your question. They may not have an answer, you may not really want an answer, but having someone validate your curiosity by listening to your question may help you find the answer yourself. And, if the first person you try to share your question with doesn't get the listening part, go to another. Don't give up until you find your perfect listener. It might be a best friend you can go to with any question or a different person for a different topic.

There will always be twists and turns on your journey. A question may get your foot on the path but don't be concerned when it leads you off the path or down another. Blaze a new path, flow with the direction and discover new questions and new answers. What fun!

It took me three years to write this little book. The conversations are real. To this day, each time I read them, I come up with new questions- not only about the words I exchanged with Virginia and Winston, but deeper, getting to know myself and heal myself questions.

If you open this book again, or share it with someone, I hope each time it helps you smile, remember, discover, and continue to question and answer your way to developing your own style of independent thinking. This direction will lead you to divine action and personal freedom. Perhaps it will help you understand more fully how and why you function as you do in relationships, decision making, and allowing happiness into your life.

It is an honor to share with you a little piece of the joy my grandchildren bring to me. Thank you for accompanying me on this adventure.

So, here we are at the end, my friends. Or is it the beginning?

Peace and love,

Nancy

*Nancy Gratta may be contacted through her website Angels by the Sea www.angelsbythesea3333.com.

The more I know,

The more I know there is more to know.

"Gammy, do you really know everything?" she asks.

"Well, almost," I reply honestly.

Printed in the United States
By Bookmasters